FOREST BOOKS

ENCHANTING BEASTS

KIRSTI KATARIINA SIMONSUURI was born in Helsinki,
has studied at the University of Helsinki and in France
and Germany, and holds a doctorate from Cambridge
University (1977). She was Senior Research Fellow at
the Academy of Finland in 1981–89, and is now Docent
in Comparative Literature at the University of Helsinki.
For 1984–86 she was affiliated with the Comparative
Literature department at Harvard University as Ful-
bright Visiting Scholar and for 1986–88 with the Depart-
ment of English and Comparative Literature at
Columbia University. Her publications include a
monograph on eighteenth-century notions of Homer
and the early Greek epic (published by Cambridge
University Press in 1979), and essays and studies on
classical and modern literature including Finnish litera-
ture. Her works in Finnish include poetry, fiction and
essays, some of which have appeared in translation in
France, the United States, Germany, Hungary and
elsewhere. She has translated Sylvia Plath, Simone
Weil and Virginia Woolf into Finnish.

&nchanting Beasts

An Anthology of
Modern Women
Poets of
FINLAND

FOREST
BOOKS
London & Boston

Edited & Translated
by
Kirsti Simonsuuri

FOREST BOOKS
20 Forest View, Chingford, London E4 7AY, U.K.
61 Lincoln Road, Wayland, MA 01778, U.S.A.

FIRST PUBLISHED 1990

Typeset in Great Britain by Cover to Cover, Cambridge
Printed in Great Britain by BPCC Wheatons Ltd, Exeter

British Library Cataloguing in Publication Data:
Enchanting Beasts: an anthology of Finnish women poets.
1. Poetry in Swedish. Finnish writers, 1900— –Anthologies
2. Poetry in Finnish, 1900— –Anthologies
I. Simonsuuri, Kirsti
839.71708

ISBN 0–948259 68 X

Library of Congress Catalog Card Number
90–71090

Forest Books gratefully acknowledge financial support for this
publication from The Finnish Literature Information Centre

Contents

Acknowledgements

Poems in this anthology have been selected from
the following collections:

MARJA-LIISA VARTIO: *Runot ja proosarunot* ('Poems and prose poems'), Otava Publishers, Helsinki 1966. EEVA-LIISA MANNER: *Orfiset laulut* ('Orphic songs'), Tammi Publishers, Helsinki 1960; *Jos suru savuaisi* ('If grief gave out smoke'), Tammi Publishers, Helsinki 1968; *Kuolleet vedet* ('Dead waters'), Tammi Publishers, Helsinki 1977. MIRKKA REKOLA: *Vedessä palaa* ('Burning in water'), WSOY Publishers, Helsinki 1954; *Tunnit* ('Hours'), WSOY Publishers, Helsinki 1957; *Ilo ja epäsymmetria* ('Joy and asymmetry'), Weilin & Göös Publishers, Tapiola 1965; *Kohtaamispaikka vuosi* ('Meeting point year'), WSOY Publishers, Helsinki 1977; *Tuoreessa muistissa kevät* ('Spring remembered afresh'), WSOY Publishers, Helsinki 1987. SIRKKA TURKKA: *Mies joka rakasti vaimoaan liikaa* ('The man who loved his wife too much'), Tammi Publishers, Helsinki 1979; *Kaunis hallitsija* ('The pretty ruler'), Tammi Publishers, Helsinki 1981; *Vaikka on kesä* ('Although it's summer'), Tammi Publishers 1983; *Tule takaisin, pikku Sheba* ('Come back, little Sheba'), Tammi Publishers, Helsinki 1986. SATU MARTTILA: *Mustan kuninkaan sydän* ('The heart of the dark king'), Kirjayhtymä Publishers, Helsinki 1987; *Tornihuone* ('A room in a tower'), Kirjayhtymä Publishers, Helsinki 1989. EIRA STENBERG: *Erokirja* ('A book of dissolution'), Tammi Publishers, Helsinki 1980; *Parrakas madonna* ('The bearded madonna'), Tammi Publishers, Helsinki 1983. KIRSTI SIMONSUURI: *Murattikaide* ('Ivy balustrade'), Kirjayhtymä Publishers, Helsinki 1980; *Euroopan ryöstö* ('The rape of Europe'), Kirjayhtymä Publishers, Helsinki 1984. *Meri, ei mikään maa* ('The sea, itself no land'), Kirjayhtymä Publishers, Helsinki 1987; *Enketlen pysäkki* ('The angel stop'), Kirjayhtymä Publishers, Helsinki 1990. TUA FORSSTRÖM: *September* ('September'), Söderström & Co Publishers, Helsinki 1983; *Snöleopard* ('The snow leopard'), Söderström & Co Publishers, Helsinki 1987. ARJA TIAINEN: *Saatanan tytär* ('Satan's daughter'), WSOY Publishers, Helsinki 1977; *Vallan Casanovat* ('The Casanovas of power'), WSOY Publishers, Helsinki 1979; *Kalastaja Merlin* ('Merlin, the fisher'), WSOY Publishers, Helsinki 1982. ANNE HÄNNINEN: *Auringonlaskun portaat* ('Sunset staircase'), WSOY Publishers, Helsinki 1980; *Tulitemppeli* ('A fire temple'), WSOY Publishers, Helsinki 1982. ANNUKKA PEURA: *Kaaoksen matkustaja* ('The passenger of Chaos'), WSOY Publishers, 1989.

Introduction

'Poetry after all in itself is a translation.'
(Joseph Brodsky, 1977)

N o poet specifically belongs to a country; yet, as most
Finnish poets, both men and women, would admit, a
poet has to explore a particular angle, a particular location of
experience that belongs to a place. A poet stands, as Mirkka
Rekola has said, 'like a narrow gate in a landscape'. Through
that gate, through that articulated perception, the whole
landscape may come into existence.

Finland's poetic tradition is full of silences, lacunae, and
sheer struggle for survival – instead of schematic continuity,
as tradition is generally seen by literary historians, there is
a singularly unified, but intermittent, poetic inspiration
that extends from the centuries-old oral tradition to con-
temporary modernism. This evolution is not paralleled by
any other present-day literature.

Finnish poetry has developed on the periphery of Euro-
pean civilization, and its off-centre characteristics are
emphasized by the fact that its language is non-Indo-
European, and that its mythology is shamanistic; but some
of its themes and motives resemble those that could be
found in the poetry of the centrally European psyche. Thus
even in the folk poetry, there are narrative poems that are
mixtures of different sources, as for instance in the
medieval cycle about the birth of Christ, where a Finnish
maiden Marjatta, a variant of the Virgin Mary, becomes
pregnant by eating cranberries (a berry in Finnish is *marja*).
In modern Finnish poetry, too, the new forms are constantly
sought after and created by the meshing together of dif-
ferent sources, different orders of experience.

To read Finnish literature has been a notoriously prob-
lematic task for foreigners. Translations from Finnish are
few, much fewer than for instance from Hungarian, a related

language of the Ugrian family. But there is a certain inaccessibility that goes beyond the literal level. To perceive this distinctive style would necessitate entering into the universe of metaphors, metonyms, and symbols that have sprung from roots other than those familiar to a European reader. Finnish language has no European history; its vocabulary as well as its deep structure flow elsewhere. It was this common history of language on which poets like Eliot or Pound could capitalize for their effects, and which truly creates intertextuality, poetic allusion, and in the final analysis, poetic tradition.

Oral literature has survived in Finland until this century. Folk poetry, of which thousands of variants survive, was sung both by men and women. Oral culture depends on memory and must be passed on through the telling of its stories, through sacred narratives and foundation myths, as well as other tales relating to the more practical level of existence. The collapse of the oral mode of maintaining cultural processes is a trauma, a source of terrible anguish and deep guilt for a culture. In Finland, the disintegration of a homogeneous symbolic universe that characterizes oral poetry has happened relatively late, in fact coinciding with the arrival of modernism, and paralleling the transition from an agricultural society to an urban, industrialized one.

Modernism arrived in Finland first in the work of Swedish-Finnish modernists, particularly of Edith Södergran (1892–1923), shortly after World War I. It is interesting to note that women poets were among the first representatives of writing that sacralized art and liberated the forms of expression such as metre, diction and syntax, as well as held poetry to be an individual expression, wanting to oppose both realism and philosophical positivism which dominated Finnish literature in the nineteenth century. Perhaps this is because lyrical poetry is by nature both private and anti-traditionalist; and both these modes are fully in the range of experience of a woman writer.

Edith Södergran has remained one of the greatest poets of twentieth-century Finnish literature, widely translated and read across the boundaries of class, gender and generation, although her work was ignored at first by the literary establishment. Her poetry depicts individual experience in raw, direct terms, yet capturing the collective imagination. It tells of a withdrawal from the world of culture and people and from discursive language, from the truth that has been defined by men. It is through such withdrawal and deliberate forgetting that she can reach her own truth, the absoluteness and purity of inward passion.

This tradition is still strong in contemporary poetry written by women. Yet, despite the undeniable female presence in Finland's literature, both oral and written, both sung and silently remembered, every poet has had to start from the beginning. Women poets are curiously much more outlawed and destitute with regard to poetic tradition and cultural crib than male writers, even now; the tradition is thinner, and the territory of unexplored subjects far wider. Each imaginative claim has expanded the availability of topics for other poets, and it is through such acts, daring or rebellious by necessity, that women poets have been able to render a complex, polymorphous reality in poetic terms, which is equally useful for male poets – for poetry does not know sex, or then, it knows them all.

Each poet in this book has added something new to the range of topics that poetry can practise; some have selected a single, special point of view, like perhaps Arja Tiainen or Anne Hänninen; some, like Eeva-Liisa Manner or Sirkka Turkka, for instance, have explored several planes of projected existence. Philosophy, history, cultural mythology, visual art, world politics, have all become subjects for poetry alongside the traditional, universal topics that relate to private experience, love, the loss of loved ones, the brevity of life, and the consolation of nature.

This anthology aims to give a multi-faceted picture of the poetry written in Finland in the 1980s. Admittedly this picture cannot be complete, for only eleven women's voices are represented. However, it is through these select visions, these individual explorations of being in the modern world, that I hope a fuller view will emerge. Reading through the poetic work of a great number of modern women poets has convinced me – as I hope it will the reader – of the vitality of Finnish poetry, even at the moment when the greatest fears of its being submerged into a multilateral, international whole are being expressed in Finland.

But a new sense of exploration and adventure can also be felt at a time when the maps of Europe are being redrawn in many places, and when history is being given back the polygenetic meaning that it has always had in the European past. These ideas can be felt in poetry even when it deals with private and intimate areas of human experience. As T.S. Eliot has said, 'the poetry of a people . . . represents its highest point of consciousness, its greatest power and its most delicate sensibility'. It is these crystallizations of thought and feeling that I hope a poetry anthology could give to a reader who may be unfamiliar with the larger context of the poems presented.

All the poets in this anthology, with the exception of Marja-Liisa Vartio who died at the age of 41 in 1966, are writing at the present day. Eeva-Liisa Manner and Mirkka Rekola made their names in the 1950s, and are generally regarded as all but classics in Finland. Sirkka Turkka, Satu Marttila, Eira Stenberg, and Arja Tiainen started publishing in the 1970s. Tua Forsström, Kirsti Simonsuuri, and Anne Hänninen began in the 1980s; and Annukka Peura published her first collection only last year.

Among the diversity of voices there are also certain similarities, and maybe a congeniality of spirit. In a certain sense, one can see resemblances between Vartio and Hänninen, both of the mythical darkness; between Manner and Peura, both explorers of invisible dimensions; between Rekola and Marttila, both of whom are poets of language. Forsström writes in Swedish, and her poetic language may have a slightly different timbre at times; her poetic psyche, however, as was the case with the Swedish-Finnish modernists of the 1920s, seems to me to be Finnish, its lyrical, imagistic space filled with forests, water, winds, and the eternal movement within. But the differences are also evident. All the poets in this book have a sense of identity that is fully their own, fully unique.

Introduction

It is for this reason that I asked each poet in this anthology to write a short preface of their own, instead of a biographico-literary introduction written by the editor. These prefaces reached me in the summer of 1990, and add to the personal and topical presences that the poems themselves demonstrate.

Kirsti Simonsuuri
Helsinki, August 1990

Marja-Liisa
Vartio

Born 11 September, 1924, in Sääminki,
died 17 June, 1966 in Savonlinna.
Several collections of poems, novels,
short stories, radio plays. Numerous
new impressions of all works.

*'During the days when I do not write, I do about the same things
as during the days when I do: I eat, sleep, and so forth.
However, I eat a lot more and there seems to be no end of need of
sleep. But when I write I sleep little. The desire to write comes
like an illness, which is impossible to cure in any other way than
going through it. When I am through it, I decide that it was the
last time. I even destroy all traces of it and feel glum.*

*A clear sign of getting better is the rising drive to clean up the
house and do the laundry. I perform a real ritual of cleaning, as
if I were driving evil spirits out of the house . . . I get enthusiastic
about all sorts of things, I make plans about studying, I feel a
fraction repentant that I have not studied plants or birds more
seriously. That task I have reserved for my old age, when I have
decided not to write. In the same way I dream about tilling the
land, about agriculture, which I find the noblest of human
occupations. The truth is and will be, however, that I get tired of
digging the tiny flower beds around my summer cottage, because
conscience beckons me to go back to writing.*

*When I write, I am perhaps like a wood grouse at mating time.
When I do not even think of writing, I am like a honey-pawed
bear that sniffs and tastes the lovely smells and berries of the
forest in order to return to its cave having eaten its food
reserves. Life is indeed a great thing, when I do not write and
when I am curious like children, to all directions!'*

(Excerpted from an article published in the weekly *Suomen
Kuvalehti*, no. 45, in 1953.)

Marja-Liisa Vartio

My green family

When did I part from my sisters, trees,
when did my green family
push me away from their circle.

Like a rolling stone,
like a grain of sand rubbing at the heels of life
I roam through highways and by-ways.

I would talk to people,
but the words are intractable,
intractable words,
that make their nests in men's ears,
that make people, hearing them, say:
Such talk is our mother tongue.

Yet my hands, my shoulders
are weary of the weight.
Words sit on them like birds,
migratory birds,
flying the spring
from hand to hand, from shoulder to shoulder.

Like a rolling stone:
so my cry begins —
but in the middle, at the moment of the deepest sighs,
the blood of my green family rises within me.
My feet split,
my arms stretch out
upwards, stiffly:
a spruce shoots   grows   arises through me,
a tree top sings and hums:
a nesting tree, a nesting tree — a rest for birds —
bringing spring, spring —

3

But when did I part from my sisters, trees,
when did my green family
push me away from their circle.
I pat   I cuddle
the brown knees of my sisters,
I stroke the shining resin hair,
when they hugging embracing
sing and sway.
They never look my way,
they don't remember me,
my family has weaned me from them.
But I lean my back along their trunks,
set my feet like they set roots in the ground,
Lift my hand as they lift branches
and I go on joining others on the way.
Not like a nesting tree, not like a watchtower —
I do not split the gales.
Only the climb   the track   the length of the back,
only the breathing of the tree tops
until the journey ends,
when the path closes,
when with a thousand hands my green family reclaims me,
with a thousand blankets muffles me
when I sleep below the song of the spruce
in my family bed.

On a windy hill

I had come alone to the hill.
Winds were asleep there, space gypsies,
squatting, with heads buried under gowns.
And even sleeping they squeezed
the keys of their accordions with bony fingers.
In flowers' arms butterflies were asleep.
Grass had set its spears crosswise.

I had travelled a long time without knowing the way,
on the edge of the same marshland, the same pond.
Nobody had heard my coming.
Only the night saw and stared, unmoving.

I told the night how hard it is to travel
without knowing the way,
how shadows startle under the spruce trees
how shadows grab your shoulders front and back,
how cold the frozen earth is, how tired I was.
I know well, I said babbling like a baby, wheedling,
I know that they are all journeying there,
those butterflies resting in flowers' arms,
those gypsies, bearing chants, those flowers,
they are all going there.
But now, when nobody listens, when all are asleep,
whisper me your counsel, tell me the shortcut to that place
where feet are soaked in cool water,
where burdens are taken and weights lifted from weary
                                         shoulders
tell it just to me.

But the night only looked, saying nothing.
Then I stretched my feet, cracked from so much travelling
I showed the bruises from trees on my shoulders.
But the night only looked without answering
only looked, although I was sobbing.

And although I had tried to speak softly, in a low voice,
    hardly moving my lips,
one of the winds rose, tapping its brothers on the shoulders,
    awakened the winds from sleep,
and as they moved, accordions broke out wailing,
drove the gypsies wildly up and down the hills,
the accordions bellowed even more terrible sounds.
The aspen woke from its dream, cold with shivers, rattling,
the flowers shook butterflies away from their bosoms,
the grass shot blindly to the air.

And there rose hands, feet, sighing, the air was thick with
    footsoles, palms, shoulders, wailing,
and they all cried out my question, they all inquired after
                                   the shortcut,
they all hammered heaven's forehead,
and my voice could no longer be heard above the others.

Three trees

Tread the earth and put out the streams,
that the hostile soil, like a needle,
a black needle,
stabs into the heels.

You stand there looking at me.

Isn't the parting on your head like the milky way,
silent, clear, and bright.

You stand there looking at me
and three trees stand around you.

Under one tree a man and a woman
hurl flowers to one another from their eyes.
Under another they turn away from each other
letting ashes flow through fingers to the ground.

But the third tree is the tallest and thickest
and in its bowers two hearts are hiding.

When the tree was young, a knife came,
cut hearts on it,
when the tree grew, the hearts on the trunk
rose ever higher.

You stand there looking at me
and the three trees around you bend upwind, humming.

And a seaful of orchids surged up,
a seaful of cotton grass moved,
many flowers grew buds on my finger tips.

What if you pressed your hand
against my silence,
if my hair flew to all four winds,
what if I rose, if I moved,
moved, inside me —

Go away, don't look back,
don't listen.
Only the seas,
the seas in me cry for their bounds.

A woman and landscape

I comb my hair this side and that,
from morning till night I comb my hair,
for the parting is not right,
for this stiff and long hair of mine
won't fall smoothly on one side of the other.
There's a mirror in my hand, but it doesn't show
my face.
The mirror doesn't give me my face.
When I raise it to eye level,
I see only a landscape,
only a mountain, water, plateau and horizon,
only black and red rivers crossing the plateaus,
only a landscape resting behind my shoulder.
I've changed places, I've sat against the airy void,
but when I raised the mirror to eye level,
there was only a landscape there.
Where could I go, I the hair-trimmer, I the mirror-holder;
wherever I went, the landscape followed
me in the mirror.

Dreams throng about me.
Dreams open gates into me.
A landscape has risen against me,
a mountain roars. A voice cries to the mountain:
                            your hunchback is coming.
Thirst has cleft her anger into shreds,
it has cut her full anger into slivers.
This coming is a humiliation,
this clinging to the feet of the mountain
this bending down to drink
from the fountain that turns rivers black and red.

Waters rest on the breast, waters press the breast.
Waters open in vast expanses,
waters raise and cradle and carry.
Someone has feet, someone has clean feet,
some have not waddled through the shore's muddy sludge.

9

And birds burst open their wings,
their wings, black on top, white under, they burst open
flying to the horizon.
One alone, that tripterous one,
falls during the journey,
on the journey always falls dead.

And clouds travel across the landscape.
The shadows of clouds travel across the landscape.
Their shadows eat into my skin
dark, burning blotches,
on my eyes they fall and my eyes fill
with bitter, vast waters.
But those waters do not find their river beds.
Those waters stand still.
Those waters stand raging still
behind the dam of my eyelids.

But the clouds roll on,
the clouds snort,
the clouds get caught in the hair of the birch.
The birch has my hair, my long and wet hair.
Like a green stream my long hair
falls on the horizon's shoulders.

Then the landscape cringes.
Then its immobile curves
straighten, scurry against —
and like a plateau I open,
like a forest I rise,
I writhe like roads and fields.
Along rivers my blood rages,
it beats in the eyes of marshes and fountains,
for the landscape has assumed my shape,
the landscape has adjusted to my outlines.

With eyes open I lie,
without moving my pupils.
Silently I lie and stare
at the vanishing point of lines that pierce me.
The sickles of lightning cut scars on my hands.
The golden and blue oxen of the sky
trample my breast with their hooves,
sharp-edged leaves fall on my face.
There is no step, no step as light
that wouldn't leave a mark on me.
They light up for the ascent, they die for the descent,
but hot ashes fall onto me,
with every touch my skin cracks.
In my black mouth I swallow the sounds
meanly I hide them within me to keep
and from side to side the tapping rolls in me,
back and forth it dashes and sways
and a cry shoots up through my breast.
It stands black and frozen.
It pricks sharply the eye of the sky.
That cry is three spruces
in the middle of a convulsed plateau.

But like a forest I rise,
like a plateau I open,
I writhe like roads and fields.
I push up trees till they meet with heaven,
with the whisper of my trees I embrace the feet of the sky
I grow around my hips a thick and bouncing grass,
a thousand ravenous root mouths gorge my breasts.
My blood I give to the orchid,
hanging black trinkets on its ankles and wrists,
when it stands with its hardened stem, full of defiance
                                        and desire
in the dusk along the roads.
My feet numb in the dew I give to the Parnassus grass,

as it lifts its black cross towards the moon.
From my finger tips I press
the hard shower of a sedge mound.

I lie with eyes open,
without moving my pupils.
Pierced by the lines I lie
and stare at the bottoms of the many-coloured boats
                                        in the sky.
And when the green bark has slid by the red one,
when the furrow of the green bark
has melted into the red furrow,
all lines break up and make a circle
and with red tongues, panting, they chase each other.
Glow worms stand to make a circle.
Like a shiny ribbon they rise up and make a circle
along my outlines on the landscape.

In the morning I made a decision: now I'll break the mirror.
Rising to my full stature I threw it to my feet.
Rising to my full anger I cried across the landscape,
I cried across all landscapes.
And from every mountain, water, plateau and horizon
I demanded me.
To every cardinal point I hurled my curses.

Did the mountain reveal its breast to the mirror,
did it grab the bottom of the waters?
Did it rip the veins from the back of the plateau's palm,
did it shake the horizon's shoulders?
The mirror lay at my feet in splinters.
From a chip a numb hand flashed;
a hand that rose, combing hair.

Eeva-Liisa Manner

Born 5 December, 1921, in Helsinki.
Over fifteen collections of poetry,
numerous prose works, drama, and
radio plays, translations of world
literature.

'The war years shadowed my youth. I was seventeen when the
Russian planes started bombarding my home town of Wiborg on
30 November, 1939, damaging it badly. At armistice, Wiborg
had to be yielded, it remained behind the border — an endless
source of nostalgia for one who had a catlike, persevering
fondness for homestead. Even as a ten-year-old, I had spine-
chilling dreams about the destruction of Wiborg, and from those
times onwards I have been haunted by reflections about the
nature and mystery of time. I believe that we have a false
conception of time; everything has already happened some-
where in an unknown dimension.

Intuitively I knew it quite early, even as a child I was a
Spinozistic determinist. Now that quantum physics has revo-
lutionized our world picture, such a belief — in fact it is an
experience — may appear hopelessly old-fashioned, but inevitably
there are fractures in determinism, just as there are ossifications
in irrationalism, in its conception of time. I have explored my
experience of time particularly in my most important collection
Fahrenheit 121 (1968). In its introductory poem I write: "I do
not believe in coincidence, at most, in the sum of chances. / Do
we have a totally mistaken notion of time / and what is about to
come, has in fact come already? / Even a dream, a vision, an
apparition will materialize / doesn't it prove that what happens/
has in fact happened already? / That the future tense is the present
tense and the present, the past tense? / That we have stuffed time
into too tight a box? / Time does not flow, is not consecutive,
but / all time is around us? / We live in a falsely co-ordinated
space?"'

Eeva-Liisa Manner

Kassandra I

Are you angry because you don't understand me?
I insult you, because you don't understand me?
Divinely inspired is my prophetic madness,
    I'm filled with it,
but I control myself and speak plainly.

Towers that you built to woo the gods
    have fallen down.
Who're you wooing now? Helen's no longer handsome.
To own female beauty, you dreamt a form for marble,
you gave stone an opaque complexion, a virgin breast,
but the eyes for ever empty repulsed you.
Whatever you achieved, you gained only emptiness.

And now, when Orpheus too is dead, thrown to animals,
head for monkeys, sex for dogs to share,
and Greek's only fit for birds,
the beasts appear,
knowing   sensing
from damp warm woods
for which he gave peace, with the music of his mind,

beasts that have broken loose from the lyre's reins
sneak like spirits into your chambers,
cry for glowing dreams on perfumed beds, in milk baths,
in the atrium, by the fountain or the book, by cool and
                      lovely style
claiming an empire. Aren't you afraid?

Kassandra II

What kind of death has given me   The yearning for
                                                                    emptiness
Fatigue made of matter   Burden that I shirk
Knowledge that makes me melancholy
Direction that nature doesn't understand

What kind of death has given me   Answer before question
What kind of death has written his words on my brain
For what kind of death do I live?

What opposite of life   For this is no life
Life is lust   energy   and excitement
beautiful   like a mad horse spurred by pain
a Macedonian mount on the Muses' mountain
when Athens is dead.

If grief gave out smoke

(for Václav Havel)

If grief gave out smoke, land would be filled with smoke.
Maybe it's already filled
and retreats to its ancient form, to the heart of night.

Conquerors come, the Middle Ages
but without medieval light:
even the sky is no longer clear.

I open it in lamplight

I open it in lamplight,
the yellowed book smells of grass and mould.

I leaf through it, a sound like rain rises
and a shallow wind goes from page to page

and over the battle field.
The bullet smoke disperses like dandelion fluff.

Noise; silence. Many horses stray around,
and men without horses. From the slit in the hatch

country sounds and smells. The shrill cry of swallows.
Anise, and wild chervil. Poppies, dandelion fluff

and on the pages of the book clouds of bullets.
The lamp's soft halo closes the battlefield.

But for the one who counts bodies

But for the one who counts bodies
    everything is one eternal doom,
she rolls around some twenty fallen
    to find her own husband or son
feeling they were all her husbands, sons.

She doesn't even cry, only rolls around.
She's losing her mind,
she begins to think, because it's impossible,
and waits for the heaven on earth,

but heaven won't come, it already came,
it was the new earth that didn't come, being too old already,
the same, and worse, than before.

Literárni Listy

Literárni Listy:
'We have not asked
other than Dubcek's government.
We continue our fight with the weapon of the word
        even though these
may be our last moments.'

That was the last issue.
Then the office was occupied,
writers and journalists were beaten
and policemen disguised as medics
took away those that had lost consciousness
        on stretchers to the ambulance.
They are worse than Nazis,
because they operate on the pretext of brotherhood,
                                        people said.
'Hitler regiert heute in Moskau', said the free
radio, and 'Alles is verloren',
and asked that it be told to others, too.

Voices. Signals. Beeps. Silence.
One asks for her husband, the other for her son.
Václav Havel, where are you now?
The Garden Party. A communiqué. A concentration camp.
Eine kleine Machtmusik.
Some say that he's dead.
At least the papers
have printed obituaries.

Puente del Rey

I drove on King's Bridge (in an earthly carriage,
with unearthly horses, like the doctor in the dream),
when the wind tossed a book roll from the eucalyptus tree,
a worm had engraved complicated news there
from right to left.
I read it like a Hamitic newspaper.
Maybe it was a Hamitic newspaper.

On the carriage a cloud fell, a thickening of mist (Dichtung),
and the writing shone more mystic than ever
when I drove on King's Way on King's Bridge
in an earthly carriage, with heavenly horses
as he, who once had replied to the false call of the night bell
and never got there.

But how can one know when the call is false?
From the fact that almost all of them are.
Except the last one, the call to a journey
which you take, not to heal someone else, but yourself,

and to read writing in reverse
in convex mirrors.

Notte, serene ombre

We walked down Spanish Steps and I
talked nonsense about the Bird playing the lute
and derailed your reason. A harlequin
might have grasped it.

And suddenly: in the north, it wasn't the evening
ploughing through the album of leaves, no trees.
Wings plough through the air and oars through water,
                                                    rotting.
Pigeons go haughty
with a lute under the arm, you see now?
Poor pigeons: only music and lice.

Night, clear shadows, the cradle of the wind,
nothing else.
For though we are together we two,
in infinity surrounded by hours
like slanting Roman numbers in the tower clock,
we are separated by a deep sleep,
the mist of crude logic, the wool of far-off fields,

around all, dead waters.

When foreseeing takes the edge off you

When foreseeing takes the edge off you,
when the room that smelled of roses and the sun is but
    a grave in the shape of a book,
when poetry is a piece of meat in the fork of a slaughterer
      or a gourmet,
when you are accused, though you don't even know the
                  passage of events,

when you're frightened of fears buried and resurrected,
when you tremble at the mirror, which at zero o'clock sharp
points at the corridors of future as long as the duration
              of hell,
when your personality is but a deep shadow,
brown as fern and grainy as old film,
taken in the past that was future,

when you're alone in the wood that shoots dark trees:
      melancholies,
when you're lost, totally lost from yourself who asks for you
at every corner like a schizophrenic echo,

and when the knight then rides past, be happy:
because he's a knight, and because he rides past.

Mirkka Rekola

Born 26 June, 1931, in Tampere.
Numerous collections of poetry, of
aphorisms. Translations, criticism and
editorial work.

'Contrasts played an influential role in my environment in all sorts
of ways, as I was growing up. I could not squeeze my real
experiences into them, nor between them. Even language was
made up of pairs of contrasts, and this struck me almost mute. My
earlier poems seem to be journeys through this predicament. A
change took place some time before the sixties. Also my idea of
power changed, power became somehow more elastic.

A poem's substance: a flock of birds that I perceived through the
train window was no more ephemeral than the rock underneath it.
I did not want to build; what I write would get built by itself, out of
my life. The polysemic nature of language has been regarded as the
hallmark of my poems. It has never been an end in itself. Language
has simply opened up experience on many levels. My books follow
from one another. A year turned into a place, why not say it, it
became like the New Jerusalem to me: time that was space.'

Mirkka Rekola

Burning in water

In water as a bait
in front of your portrait
silver, flowing
quickly, glowing.

Do you see the double
fishes afire.
Your eyes kindle.
Burning in water.

In sunlight

The moon crescent remained till daylight.

We have a longing for what used to be.
We want to reclaim
the stars and our dark-blue night.

Here

One that grew, fell.
A wanderer falls on a stub.
The crown came down
the branch was robbed of its breeze.
Come now, road, and settle here.
You did not say a thing before.
The axe has been carried home,
my forest sold.

In my place

My eye is ever shadowed by a hawk.
I fear the quick blow
nor am I wrapped in cabbage leaves
here I am
sunk among the slender trunks.

I say there are quite a few
sharp lines going by
they must fly
for I'll stay here
the shadow will change forever.
Or it will land in me, the wind bird
shooting its shadow in the end
with beak ajar.

I left for the lakes

I left for the lakes
    I wouldn't disappear from your eyes
I left for the lake
    I lie awake
around the moon
my oar always always
strokes your vaulted eyebrows
    beloved

the lake is dark
you sleep   the same dark in your eyes

Pine needles

Pine needles in the sun ball.
Quiet in the grass, it doesn't smell   doesn't fall off.

In early summer
the hedgehog jumped to a tarpit.
It was a hedgehog.

Here grew a little thirst and a lingonberry.

Autumn rainfalls

Autumn rainfalls piano lessons
leaves   in flocks   birds
bow and violin in a case
past wet tree trunks
afternoon and passers-by
under horizontal boughs
birds   in flocks   leaves
face always on the road.

In a train in a tram

In a train in a tram
in a bus in a plane
in a store in a café
it is quiet to read

A chair stood there

A chair stood there so that I could sit
and wonder from where I came here:
a world   a room   a sheet of paper
like a circle, quartered.
I left, let the door go first, it gave way,
the blank wall, to my writing hand.
I saw the leaves of the trees
and the leaves of the trees were about to come out
in the park a girl whose leg danced sideways
blue in the eyes throughout the land
     Joy and Asymmetry.
The sky resounded
blue, in the eyes, throughout the land
a seagull on the back of a seagull and spring.

Who hid inside our couple

Who hid inside our couple, couldn't do otherwise,
made an experiment out of her life,
and no one, by forgetting, nor by any other nonchalance,
                                                    could
harm her any more
than she harmed herself, at most taking
her temperature, if there was one, if for that reason she'd
stopped urinating.
She saw through and heard through, no wonder then
that the world unfolded.

I went around in a round house

I went around in a round house
anti-clockwise
driven by windows   by sealight
       to a cool table.
Looking towards the sound, I ate there.
Sailboats in curtains,
       masts sparking
the banner flushing.
   I leaned on my hand,
a small motor boat about to start
sweeping a circle.
This is the same house around which I went in winter.
I saw your face outside,
   I saw you right there against dandelions
against sea,
this is the house,
   I thought of the year,
such an open one, in the windows of the sea.

Aphorisms

Man, standing there like a narrow gate in a landscape.

Feeble, he lived with all his strength.

They talk about you behind your back, there they remain.

You need a scapegoat, you get it, and it kicks you.

You win time from children, don't you understand.

Man's helplessness was so great that birds began to fly.

Sirkka Turkka

Born 2nd February, 1939, in Helsinki.
Nine collections of poetry, prose volumes.
Head stableman and librarian. Finlandia
Prize in 1987.

'The summer has been windful in places and the crust of the lake behaved accordingly. The window of my lodge faces the shore where trees dangle their branches. It is raining now, more than that I cannot say. In this small room, bed clothes, books and old letters are floating. I am floating in life, which I do not comprehend. The dog is my friend, that I comprehend. I enter the forest and stare at gigantic blueberries, just as if a thousand solar eclipses were looming from the midst of the mossy ground. Behind the cottage, on the slope of a hill, there are large mossy stones: I have looked at them for twenty years and hoped that they would hold out, and fare well.

The whole summer my typewriter has been standing on the table by the window. Not even once have I removed its cover, let alone written anything. I hear that I am a poet of the first rank. I do not know what is being manifested in me.'

Photo: Pertti Nisonen

Sirkka Turkka

Los Angeles and the defence of angels

Los Angeles and the defence of angels. Ahead
long winter days, street cars.
There's a hole in the second mailbag at Annankatu Post
Office
and on winter days, dogs
do drillings in the snow,
for nothing, without thanks.
Exalting this life, a poet foams in a café.
After the well-known war novelist
had blitzed himself to death,
he became the first in the trade. I rise
and yell: *We shall overcome, yeah.*
A ball of slush, like the snowdrop lost in the snow,
in the street, congruent vessels
with rain cloaks on their shoulders, transparent.
I couldn't always bear myself, the artillery fire
against the gist of beauty, cyanide moon, rain, hovering
stage-sets, there comes a point
where I always give up.
Without a memory I came to the world, without a mind
I leave this place, I'm not in the least loyal.
I do not let others pull
the carpet under my feet,
I'll do it myself.

Stars are again like a teary ballad

Stars are again like a teary ballad, and at nights
dogs tune their cloven violins.
I do not let sorrow come,
I do not let it near.
A thousand feet of snow over my heart.
I mumble a lot to myself, in the street
I sing aloud.
Sometimes I see myself in passing, with a hat, perfect food
for winds, with some thought or other aslant.
I talk about death, when I mean life. I walk with my papers
in a mess, I don't own a single theory, only a swearing dog.
When I ask for liquor, I'm offered ice-cream,
I may be a Spaniard, with my hairline
low like this, indeed:
I may not be from these parts.
I sweat, trying to talk, once and a while
I tremble.
Almost more than for my death, I mourn for my birth.
And all I ask for
is a thousand feet of snow over my heart.

In the forest of hooves

In the forest of hooves, in the forest of horsehair, he sleeps
inside the tree the deep sleep of the tree.
Here the wind blows from sea to sea
and at nights the moon is two slender knees
that glow side by side!
The mad horses of the night
are loosened from their halter, thighs
press against their flanks like love
that won't give, won't open, won't yield
anything from itself.
In the dusk the wind moves, a lime tree plant
wanders in the dark still, not knowing
of love that won't give of itself.
One that won't consent, even if
the whole dark sky of the night
and the manure mounds steaming in the dawn
begged it.
Inside the forest of horsehair he sleeps,
clinging to love amidst lean moon knees.
Clinging to love that robs days and seasons
of their names, and won't even let the snow rest.
That won't give, won't yield
but withholds,
won't caress, won't mitigate.
And though the thickets now get lighter
at the corners of the night, love won't
loosen, the gate won't open.
He's asleep, bruised with love
so without himself.
All nights and moons,
asleep, never resting.

Before death itself arrives

Before death itself arrives,
it paints pine trunks all red
around the house.
It lifts the moon to the sky, a bright moon,
on its side, like an old vessel,
cracking at its enamelling of light
above this house where the night
now folds together.
And as the currents of water embrace and alternate,
the house slowly gets ready, all by itself,
for death.
Even long before death arrives,
moon mountains rise and fall
above the tiny house that was home,
crouching, breathing inaudibly.
The hinge of the night turns, the moon leaves
returning again.
I club a cross on the door and on the wall,
to the snow and to the trunk,
I light a wax cross
so that the guest may come.
Night, a wave chases a wave
night, the ebb and low of the snow.
Night, sweet-scented sheets and pillow cases
swell into sails, in anticipation,
on their journey from the rib cage to the earth,
to a resounding frozen earth.
You cannot stop on that road,
you cannot look behind, you
cannot hollo towards the front.
The heart may roll like little rugs
by the gate post, glow
like carnations against the snow's skin.
You, too, get ready, little bush,
licking my window with black flames.
Get ready and be prepared.

44

For death is kind
when it comes.
It holds you against its breast.
Wordless, it lets you know your childhood lullaby,
bringing it to you behind your bent back,
from beyond years, decades.
It gives a gift to your childlike hand, a gift
that you keep looking at with bleary eyes.
It gives you the song you thought you had forgotten.
Its shoulders and breasts are covered with flowers.
It is hollow, in order to take in the whole being.
It grabs you by your edges.
It spreads you out:
it tries to understand you.
And then it has grasped.
It nails your eyes open,
opens your mouth, from where
the tumult of life is escaping.
And you look, no longer at me,
but through me
beyond me
to your own death.
And to the white flowers
that have blossomed
around the tiny house.

Your time of wine and roses

Your time of wine and roses
    has gone away
when your beautiful beloved
    leaves you.
When he leaves you
    the rose is so lonely,
the wine, like a sculpture in a glass.

For love is just a stranger

For love is just a stranger.
    And I tie my emptiness
around you like a skin, my own darkness,
    all that is beating and heavy.
Winter comes and gazes like Valentino,
    feeling softly with his paw
like the lion of the publican Rousseau.
And from here, from the land of shadows,
    from the land of snowy shadow I cry for you,
        not like for God
            but like for my one and only
                my sole life,
    this body, a thicket of bones that hides
        in its dusk slumbering opaque organs,
        a heart like a struggling rose.
And look: when the rose has sprung back
        it has sprung back
    and the red cardinal colour
        has dropped its petals.
    Winter has come
and night fallen.

Life is a house swaying in the wind

Life is a house swaying in the wind
  with hop bine rambling round walls and stairs,
   laughter round a quick sob.
The house must be sold quickly before it falls,
   its rooms already let out foul speech.
How I miss you at times, when the lightning fills
  the sky, you're like Venice in December, when it rains.

Your neck is a barn door, a church wall,
  it narrows upwards when one looks from below,
   when you stand on a ladder, hitting a nail.
And the nail, too, reaches to the sky
    and the sky to infinity, this will never end,
   a knife has now been struck through the heart
   like the nail through the sky.
These houses must be sold, I think, buildings,
   and I think of how by Sannäs
    the hens always cross the road
  and the poplar trees stand in a row
   like pious little boys.

And I want that you

And I want that you
    finally would tremble,
when the lake, wet from rain
    lifts the summer on its wings,
        lifting the swans.
When they halt for a little while yet
    above park trees, above
    all beloved gold.
When their colour is
    even whiter than snow,
whiter than the colour of resolution.

Satu
Marttila

Born 12 March, 1941, in Helsinki. Six
collections of poetry, editorial work.
Poetry programmes for the Finnish
Broadcasting Company. Poetry editor
at a Helsinki publishing house.

'I write, therefore I am. Making a poem involves identity.
Writing, giving birth to a poem is difficult, impossible, slow,
excruciating, and yet: the overwhelming joy that creative work
can give you in its course, is beyond comparison. Where does the
subject matter come from? How does a poem come into this
world? There are no answers to these eternal questions, for the
answers lie hidden in the bottom mud of consciousness, in the
depth of subconscious darkness, to where a word casts its
crushing light and reveals what has crept onto paper: a poem.

It is easier to talk about the powerful sources of creative
writing than about the actual creative process. Ever since I was
quite young, nature has given me comfort and visions, it has
been filled with life that can be verbally animated, it has yielded
beauty and devotion, wonder and delight, it has allowed a pan-
theistic entering into, and above all – as for instance in my
collection "The Heart of the Dark King" – it has offered itself, so
to speak, as the mental and lyrical stage of strong love experiences.
Love themes occupy a central place in my work. Mythical
nature themes have also become more intimately felt there. For
me, a poem is, to a large extent, a whole that is sung; Finnish
folklore has influenced my idea of poetic language. I have a
passionate love relationship with words; my favourite reading is
the etymological dictionary.

I have two grown-up children. I share my life with my loved
one and with my cat.'

Photo: Jorma Wartiovaara

Satu Marttila

Mulled wine

Mulled wine the colour of your lips,
veins afire, a restless bird
in the breast's bony cage, my cry
responding to your whisper,
the precious goblet of your hips
in my hands I bear
like the one life.

When you look

When you look,
the glow of wild flowers goes out
this meadow fallen asleep on a summer evening
turns into marshland,
look, look
from the swampy pit a dark rose will rise.

The wells of your eyes

The wells of your eyes reflect a forest,
I wished to get lost in there, and I found
a herb Paris in the moss.
Don't guide me back towards people,
the secret lies in the berry's taste.

Throw over me the dark cloak

Throw over me the dark cloak of the night, open
the tinkling buckles, and the dark vest,
hothand, pick from the skin's snow
the memory of virginity,
take me to black woods, to the damp
valley of wolves, to a wolf snare
filled with panting,
tearing apart, happiness.

You wolf, you rainmaker

You wolf, you rainmaker,
pearls fall from my heaven,
rain pearls on to your fur
you wolf, I'm your bride,
but beware the slithery silk, mother of pearl,
teeth hide inside there.

An account book

So much is missing from the account book
of times past: so many tears,
so many trips taken in vain,
permissions sought and wishes made.
was it so little I had time to give them,
bedtime tales of the unnecessary and no use,
didn't I tell them of the bending birch branch
resting against the solitary night cloud
like a hand on the cheek of a sleeping lover,
didn't I tell them of the billowing blue of the lilac
storming like the sea of happiness,
didn't I tell them of the summer day vanishing tomorrow
or of the lake's constant eye
clear like the tear in mine
when I go through the heavy accounts,
give my wavering hand to times past.

Houses

I rest my head on to the lap
of silence and, in the small hours, recall
the sleepy smell of the dark room,
arms aglow from the day,
locks of hair glued onto the apple cheek,
the innocent shadow of an eye lash.
I recall the games played to the end,
set theory and the scab on the knee,
the yellow bicycle that was stolen.
I recall lego houses, whose pieces
the hoover's greedy mouth gobbled inside the dust.
Already they are building the house of tomorrow,
youth, on whose forehead the morning shines.

The children of Mother Moon

Mother Moon, Bathing Woman, in vain
you call and keep awake,
you won't find your children any more, we have
gone already along the far water routes,
in vain you call your children
on a star-lit night,
we have other names already,
we're now travellers-in-water,
with shiny metal scales we swim
out of the windows of a sunken palace
in whose holes the sleepy hairs
of seaweed flutter and flow.
Mother Moon, Bathing Woman, in vain
you look for us, we won't come back any more,
we're fishes now, crown-heads, we swim
out of the palace gates where
the slow tanks of jellyfish guard,
we swim with beaming sides
to the green sea of life,
we swim with reddish fins,
carrying a huge message on our lateral lines.

An old song

Night has sunk behind the window
and the cat has rolled in his sleep.
I listen to an old tune
about encounter and departure,
about the heart's great fire,
about love and sorrow.
In the old song they say
you're on your way to me.

Ad astra

Rotting leaves, earth smell,
the night sky above the musty marshland,
a heavy cloth and its golden embroidery.
From the deepest earth
I reach out my hand
towards the still unwoven
constellations of happiness.

Eira
Stenberg

Born 8 April, 1943, in Tampere. Five
collections of poetry, novels, radio
plays, children's books and plays.
Studied at the Sibelius Academy,
works as a freelance writer.

*'Poetry is the well of Narcissus that reflects the face of Medusa:
love and death have presided over its birth. At the backdrop of
art there looms a loss, both one that has really happened and
those chances that life has denied. And in the final analysis, a
loss that is the most merciless: one's own death. But the pain
that gives birth to a poem, springs from love. An artist is
possessed by an unusually strong will to live and an awareness
of her own uniqueness. My fear of death is the fear of being
buried alive, the revolt against the fact that life will not allow
the realization of all possibilities. And exactly that, life won't
allow. Even the fact of having been born a woman or a man
predestines the lot that denies the other alternative.*

*I feel that writing is, at bottom, a kind of deep narcissism: it
means a love relationship with oneself, and as is always the case
with love, the whole spectrum of feelings is displayed within it.
A poem is Orpheus's call to Eurydice to come back to life, its
purpose is to sing the dark side of one's self, to become alive. It is
an internal act of love where the different sides of one's persona
passionately seek one another. It requires courage, as love does,
and skill and patience to search out the right words that would
move the sovereigns of loss.'*

Eira Stenberg

Slowly I slide your hand

Slowly I slide your hand off my skin
slowly the warmth leaves —
I'm getting cold.
As a mole I dig through the years,
past rusty weapons
until I find
a stone-carved sign.
I amass a museum around me
in order to muffle you.
And yet your face returns
like an image on the surface of water
after a useless stone.
I have pushed you away
in order to dream.
For otherwise I can only love
unhappily.
I have been condemned to kiss a face
that I have made myself.
How pitiful I've become.

We made our nest in an old tree

We made our nest in an old tree
joyfully we were wedded.
Nobody invited grief
as a guest of honour,
we didn't know that grief needed to be entertained,
the past lamented,
for usually it comes uninvited
just at the wrong moment.

They waited on the branches, croaking:
we had made our nest in a family tree.
It was a jungle
disguised as flesh, dropping raw fruit.
When chance ran through the leaves,
mothers, fathers, kids,
a gruesome cry and strife filled the room.

Yet on its trunk there'd been carved a heart.

Mounds have fallen

Mounds have fallen in the crevices on the floor.
The forgotten begins to sprout.
The seeds of pomegranate trees have burst
from their shells and a strange mirage rises
from the midst of furniture.
So true it is
that parrots land on the branches
and we must listen to a voice that repeats
incessantly

> if you didn't
> if you could
> if only some time

For a moment I dreamt

For a moment I dreamt:
we'd kiss so
that teeth would fall out!
We'd begin from the start
like infants.

An impossible thought.
Who would nurse us?

A cranky five-year-old

I took two rings from the drawer,
two haloes of a lilliput
and put them back to my nameless ring finger.
I needed to rest my hand:
the ring finger weighed like a cranky five-year-old
refusing to walk any further.
It had two names: You and I.
The family name was at a loss, balancing feet.
The finger was nameless for a moment.
An arrow shot from the past, piercing my breast.
I took shelter behind the typewriter
it banged far worse than a machine gun.

Good-bye my lilliputs,
I remember Gulliver's fate.
I am on my way out already.

From autumn mists the everyday

From autumn mists the everyday comes rushing in
like a perch from the cold reeds
(oh finland my land my finland).
Bonjour tristesse, welcome distress
welcome you coughing one, you with a runny nose
whose nooks pile up with paper hankies,
welcome skirts that do not flirt
welcome blues
allowance roulette   bills   account in the red
welcome you autumn which sprinkles
gold without a hallmark
welcome old storm that makes me grab my hat
welcome penny-stretching   door-bolting   frozen smiles
staring at feet, and at puddles
(welcome my land my finland).

A bearded madonna

A bearded madonna has been painted
at St. Sophia's in Ohrid.
My well-informed Macedonian friend tells me:
the painter thought
it was Christ he had to paint
forgetting then to remove Mother's beard.
How I admire human wisdom:
nobody wanted to kill
a child's dream.

Kirsti
Simonsuuri

Born 26 December, 1945, in Helsinki. Five collections of poetry, novels, essays. Scholarly works, translations of world literature, criticism, editorial work. University teacher and researcher.

'The blood of an exile and a vagabond flows in me, as a poet; in my work I seem to be looking for the restlessness and peace that is in life itself. For many years, for most of the seventies, I was deeply alienated from my mother tongue. I rediscovered it at the same time as I found my lyrical space again, my own natural way of moving within it. To be without one's mother tongue for a while can be beneficial for a poet, because it heightens the awareness of the specificity of one's own language among other languages. To live in other cultures can help a writer to perceive the eternal movement between otherness and sameness. This is the experience of our century. People who live in exile, ideas and images that shift and enmesh, nations that migrate, are re-charting the world that we know. I believe that poets are everywhere messengers of the future without a permission.

Something propelled me into going even when very young. The symbolic and metaphoric nature of the world was the theme of my meditations and I wanted to try out the boundaries of my understanding. Sometimes my poems are like the reflected re-portage of these experiments; sometimes I exist beyond my poems and my language, in the region where I do not yet know and where I could just as well be dreaming. Maybe for this reason I have used dream material: there I am face to face with a universal structure, similar to which I find when I study ancient cultures, or wander in the world, among different people. I would not want to be afraid of anything. But when I notice that I am afraid of something, I am forced to rethink everything, from the beginning. The future is a facet of the present. And the rest is trying to find the right words.'

Kirsti Simonsuuri

Mother tongues

Then came solitude cool   remote
away from the hell of others
I alone I spoke in all tongues
      forged keys to secret codes
      sweet water: Latin
      wild strawberry: Finnish
my silence was as deep
as in the womb, once

A monk

I lock my bicycle to a balustrade, an ivy balustrade
and all the tomes in the cathedral library
say nothing
            iron chains, rustflakes
my days are chained down
my life in the carrel
the whole world and the morning's
barbs in my throat, eyes, ears
on my lips the name of the nightmare
fiend, everything is possible
on this morning of limits

My hand opens the lock
            a golden lock
the writing opens itself
            golden writing opens
I've driven this road for centuries
from far-off centuries
the holes in the granite are the floor's eyes
they can see you coming
I don't know how far they can hear
            it's midsummer
            and pears are ripening

Travelling light

It is as though I saw it all
diminished to the core
the whole day to a minute
the suitcase to a book
the long conversation to a word
looks of longing to a smile
and hopeless choice to what must be
it is so light, so clear
I want nothing more anymore
          only wind stroking waves
          onto a distant shore

Arctic journey

Fog only makes this emptiness vaster.
What I see is the window, my own face,
cold that congeals my eyes is what I see.
I remember believing, when I was a child,
the world ended at Hammerfest,
the earth came to an abyss
and there was just fog beyond;
that's what I believed.
I've come north because something
in me was finished, I'm dead weary,
compass gone, its needle constantly
wandered, it's been lost in the snow.

        If only I could hear a ship's horn hooting
        in the fog out there, I'd find my way.

Night opens three roads

Night opens three roads:
death, peace, and love.
Do not take peace
it will end in death.
Do not take love
it will end in peace.
Take death
it is the best, it will end
in love.

At the door

In March blow the winds, today the trees
    bend, and the wooden houses sigh
        on their foundations, we live in them,
    in their core, as inside ships
          people's lives
    is to live in voyaging ships
      that glide along the streets
        amidst cars, dogs, tall maple trees
I ask what is their address.
And children run from giants' gates
    grown-up houses won't unlock,
        they don't even hear the knock, but
          the day when I stepped from the stream
you received me, at the villa's heart.
        We don't know to whom we open our doors,
          when life begins
    we don't know if it's a poet or a child that comes,
    we don't notice; and quite unawares
        the one we love is at the top of the stairs
wearing a blue jacket.
In Moscow a funeral takes place again
    almond trees are blossoming in Rome
    behind the ocean the sun has risen
    but the world is created wherever we are,
      at dawn we open all windows and doors,
winds blow, hurrying for departure.

Moving

House-moving all morning:
everything topsy-turvy
people passing through rooms
along stairs, through doors.

Around noon
a stranger takes the tables
that talked yesterday, are mute today
objects turned into objects
furnishings for a strange hotel.

On the landing
the dark man with white hair
lets the heavy sideboard and
loveseat parade past
down the staircase.
Now tripod forms are
merely numbers on men's shoulders.

Why are they going, leaving home
riding off in trucks
to other houses
making this vacancy?

I look at the cabinet
with its little Corinthian-column legs.
That goes, too, its past
no longer holds it
everything's been freed
the house moved.

Night in Manhattan

A reed bows and dies, walls sway
people bend and life falls
upon them, mute feathers fly away

Walls are linen, hairlike
rising from skulls on gluey reliefs
and break up in the gleam of neonlights

Man has nested in the canyon of garbage bags
built his peace among rodents
and bitten poison from black plastic

A dusty cage yells: help me or fuck off
help me or I kill, and barely rises, floating
inside the bag, a glowing fragile ball

Eyes burn a hole in the molten ash
the reed bows and inside the bag
blows the wind, void, sleep's broken breath.

The garden of earthly delight

As Bosch looks with his painter's brush
into the garden of earthly delight
deeply, like a hawk, in detail,
and from the round glistening membrane of the eyes
reflects a glass ball, the words
of lovers, a closed world where hands,
one resting on the thigh, the other on the belly
measure the vibration of thought on the skin
and feel the blessed echo of conception:

Happiness creates phrases that withdraw
into a glass ball, when a garden grows
inside there, when speech encapsulates
one world and responds to another
outside the glass.
It's far from the glass shell to another planet
through empty space, through language without signs,
when imagined reality, the created world
floats inside the glass ball, in Bosch's painting.

Tua

Forsström

Born 2nd April, 1947, in Porvoo.
Writes in Swedish. Seven collections
of poetry, plays, editorial work.
Literary editor at Söderström & Co.

'I have always written out of a nervous, rather over-active state of mind where it feels as if I had no language whatsoever. A little as if one were on a trip, not knowing what is said around one. One of our cats shot off to the woods and remained absent for two months. When I found him, he behaved oddly; he ran like a lunatic up my trouser leg, scratched me, miaowed and growled. Suddenly I realized that he tried to show fidelity, but was mistaken about its expression. After some days he came and again stroked himself against us. I was taken by this, I thought I recognized myself in it. I write what I only just can, not necessarily what I want to. It is no good to try to please in poetry, that shows immediately. I believe that one must write free of personal feelings of prestige; one cannot present oneself as higher, purer, more liberated than one is.

On the other hand, naturally I cannot know what a cat remembers. But this question of remembering and forgetting interests me very much; it seems that the one overlaps with the other and vice versa. Memory is after all an idiosyncratic room, which is furnished inside and out in various ways. Sometimes one pulls sheets over the armchairs, it stands there empty and seemingly unused, sometimes one moves in there in full light and it is a feast. We change, everything changes with terrific speed, one cannot go back to something, for one has already become another. At the same time it is our capacity to remember and to forget that makes us into what we are. Yes, we consist of our memories and of our hopes, just as we consist of water and molecules. There is little distance between memory and dream, these secret rooms where everyone can uphold a dignity.'

Photo: Leif Rosas

Tua Forsström

The crazed geography and time

The crazed geography and time
of all transit halls, the electric
stream   an epileptic attack   Mechanically
I move myself in fits towards Helsinki,
back there. Home. Mindlessly babbling
bodies, missing   stinking Dioressence and the businessmen
lapping   drinking here with a nervous nonchalance: small
false moves, starts: whereto whereto . . . ?
Sudden bickering breaks out among
the ones who leave and see off
But me then! Me! I will not! I want to
have it all, at once!
Travel as the sense of travel, escape as way
of keeping images intact?
I long for somewhere else.
I long for my oligotrophic sea.
In the life of someone who travels maybe chance
becomes the invariant, foreign
sites familiar like   dreams
I'll make sure that I've learnt
nothing. A stormy night brought St. Christopher
the small child from the stream

Then it had been March

Then it had been
March. To sleep in a room head north in a bed
with one's nose in someone's gruff
frock that smelled of leather, thyme,
melted snow, a Man
like an Asiatic market. 'It gets
on the nerves', said Lenin listening to
the Appassionata, 'It makes one talk
nonsense rather than hit men on their heads'
Towards evening the snow crust became quite blue.
I think that with you I travel
wherever. You say: do with me
whatever you want.

Day resembled night

Day resembled night, like the bottom of the sea shadowed
by a quick cloud seen through green transparent water
Yes, to mean is as if to go towards another.

It's a long time since I was a little girl

It's a long time since I was a little girl
I'm a little girl who goes round and round here
A long time ago my little dolly on a chamber pot
read a book of poems. Truth goes high and low
It's a long time since these mouldy rooms
were inhabited, nonsense, it's a long time since I was
unloved!
There hangs a thick humming grizzle of rain
over the surface of the water
We must live as if nothing happened.
It is as if we waited for the neighbours or
the police to knock at the door and say: Follow me
Yes, as if nothing happened, aseptic, as if
the ultimate days were something personal
For you I was quite unprepared, as for an illness.
Here. Arrest me. Confiscate it all, my
clothes. Throw me into that jail
by the subterranean sea.

Foliage reflected in the eye

Foliage reflected in the eye, a broken neck
depict what it's like to be a bird and fly
towards foliage reflected in the glistening sky:
a muddled memory of the joy of falling
to a meeting with someone so like one's self

In photographs

In photographs your eyes
are a fraction
asymmetrical, there is
no formula
for men. Water
and light oddly spaced out
Fractures, fantasy.
Nakedness. Innocence and crime.
A rondo flowing from one of
the inner chambers: something fulfilled
and inevitable
'In order to live in the world
one must found it'
I slip open an envelope
with a knife, newly-mown grass
steams in through the window
An instantaneity!
In slow processes!
I say I regret it all
I regret nearly all, it
plays no role
I knew you even
as a child as I thought like a child
Yes, water and light.
Cracks in the base.
Inflammations.

It is as it is

It is as it is.
It may appear
helpless.
It is helpless.
Act only according to
instructions, avoid
hysteria. Avoid
anorexia nervosa. In the beginning
one cries a lot, not wanting
to be a mistake and Fleurs
du Mal. One begins to get on.
Someone stretched himself
naked and didn't want it.
Someone let it happen.
One receipts dispatches
that contain darkness quarried
out of darkness in another locale.
One reports oneself as missing.
One reports oneself as wounded.
I held someone tightly
in my mouth until it
flew over.

It rains sand and cinders

It rains sand and cinders

One day one comes out maybe on the other
side, in the cool reading rooms

Someone spills me out like water

They come out in twilight

They come out in twilight, sprawling
shadows over a field. They share
a measure of pig, badger and fox. Helplessness
is their foremost characteristic. They rootle in snow
for something to eat. We find them unnatural:
their pointless vagrancy, hunger, their obscene
lack of self-defence. In danger, the raccoon lies down
pretending to be dead. We find such behaviour
pitiful, the pitiful we find repulsive, we're
shocked by these starving shadows
of the sugarbeet field, so different from the snow leopard
that silently pursues his prey six thousand feet
above sea level.

Arja
Tiainen

Born on 19 October, 1947, in Seinäjoki,
Ostrobothnia. Nine volumes of poetry,
two prose works, columns, criticism.

*'I experience myself strongly as a thinker; or rather: an anti-
thinker, an almost-thinker. Although I am poet of a small
country, there are no boundaries in the realm of poetry. Soul
travels. Most often, my mind is occupied with role games, old
myths, the woman's obstacles and the laws of the male world. In
my own country I am regarded as a violent, even an aggressive
poet, but that is a superficial view. Many stories of my poems
reflect fundamentally quite romantic situations; besides, the
hero of my love poems is almost always male. I'm only defending
freedom of speech and expression, always and everywhere. I
loathe everything small and petty. I draw the lines of my poems
with a metallic hand. Perhaps I am a fighter, a fighter for art.*

*Yes, my education is nil. I come from a large family of war
immigrants who could not educate all their children. Besides, I
was, and still am, word-blind: that was catastrophic at school.
Now I train basenjis. I am divorced and have one child. And I do
not feel bound to any time or place. I have a strong feeling of
solidarity with the lyrical poetry of the entire world.'*

Photo: C.-G. Hagström

Arja Tiainen

The beautiful rider

With me you'd have the time of your life,
nobody's ever complained, they all
want it all over again, why don't you, just once?
        You could screw me whatever way you please
I'd pretend to be a piece of meat in a skewer,
like a worm in a hook, like a cake in a mould,
elastic, wonderful, quiet
        or wild, those tricks.
Wonder why you're not interested?
I'd be a Jolly Mattress That Sings.
Or: a rambler, creeping, insatiable.
A boat in the surge. A beautiful Rider.
An eel hung in the ceiling, naked, lovely.
A wide aperture, a rolling Night of Joy.
A sighing tree, a two-tongued mouth, eyes,
        I'd eat you up at once
I'd tear you apart, I'd claw you all bloody,
        I'd leave monstrous marks
                or wouldn't.
Why won't you fuck me?

Adolescent men

Adolescent men, always
seeking refuge in a woman, grabbing
the sleeve, the glass, the gun, the knife, regretting
giving up, leaving things half-done,
shrugging shoulders at life, sticking
a note at the window, burning bridges before
new ones have been built,
plunging into a woman's womb,
crying for mom, what a mistake, what a dreadful mistake.
And nothing is left for women,
     no one to trust and find shelter, no one
but themselves. No other role
but the mother's, the caretaker's, the comforter's role.
That species of man is dangerously increasing.
One cannot even enjoy them in bed.

A full-time woman

Won't you ever take up being a full-time woman,
it's nothing but menstruation cycles
pills and IUD's, make-up instructions
all abracadabra,
home-made sweetbread and floors
without a scrap, going from one special offer to another.
Living at the mercy of hearsay and chance.
You always have to be
some buttress, waiting with a memo in hand
what comes and why won't it yet.
A pair of mammary glands that can clean the house.
    Sheet laundry is the fate.
Service is fine but what about the socks and panties?

Some women are pillars

Some women are pillars in the hall,
radar stations, lie-detectors.
But what is it that keeps them in place themselves
except a blatant or hidden lie?
In order to live, even truth sometimes
has to spread its chaste legs, pretending at least
a genuine orgasm.

Good people?

Good people? Wasn't it they who
walked without question to concentration camps.
Good people? Isn't it they who get trampled,
exploited, locked up in asylums.
Tell me how far have people got
by goodness or empathy.
No further than to a boring marriage . . .

And suddenly everything becomes lovable

And suddenly everything becomes lovable, the blue sky,
the worn books on the shelf, and how the sun paints golden
flowers forgotten in a vase,
a glass of milk on the table —I go through in my mind
the history of humanity, a fish crawling ashore from water,
beginning to gasp for air, lizards, brontosauri
shaking the cloud-covered earth, and what caused their end,
a sudden ice age, a comet, a massive meteorite?
Man devours raw meat in dark antiquity,
begins to till the soil and make war?
Always new and better, more efficient weapons.
Always a thousand reasons to conquer and beat the enemy?
And I feel sorry for Europe, now being threatened
from all quarters, as if it were already
     just a target.
We must imagine a better end for us.

Hurry up

Hurry up: Venus on the morning sky, reach your hand
so that the sun won't cover it, reach your hand
    for eleven years we've been waiting
like donkeys for donkey's years, waiting in line like planets.
A miracle, if love then didn't blossom, seas, tides
wouldn't surge over us . . . I'll smear him with wine and
                                      honey,
lick every inch of his skin
— each second is dear, now take off your clothes,
fold on the chair those barriers that we've been wearing
damn the rows of buttons, walls of zips, calendars
that would hate our love,
there's no time to waste, now that finally I can
taste you without the cold camera eyes, without snoopers,
without love police that pry at our acts
having no idea what they might be.
Venus on the morning sky, you at an arm's distance from me
what a fiery spiral: I don't know where it will take us
    when we're now stars in the same constellation,
speak to my ear of the pain and the beauty.

Anne
Hänninen

Born 7 February, 1958, in Rautalampi.
Five collections of poetry. Freelance
writer and teacher.

'I grew up in Central Finland, in the countryside, with my grandparents. Nature is precious to me, and its significance for me has become wider: it is a timeless, eternal power, the core. A well of responses, endless variations, symbols. I cherish this world, this lost world, I build it anew: this sense of freedom, union, understanding, existence.

I think that the language of poetry comes closest to what life is. Ordinary language is limited: you cannot speak poetry. My poems are born in different ways. For instance: there is a racking conflict, an unruly tendency to wonder, to question, to doubt, to dig, to suffer. Or: there is an overwhelming enthusiasm, wild flow of words, inspiration, a lit-up joy. Or: there is a completely emptied feeling, a vacuum, a wordless, embarrassed, aimless state. And suddenly something new and unexpected begins to flow into it. Sometimes, a sensation of the divine, of beauty, of meaning in the midst of fear and chaos. And I try to find words that might be even a little equal to the nuances of existence, of uniqueness, of fluidity. And on no account imitation, repetition.

But how difficult it is to blow the spirit into words. To try to capture something immaterial with words. To try to arrest a vague fluctuation, to become conscious.

One can try to create a world through poems; through the magic of words, of creation songs, of incantations. To tame what is strange. I also want to make documents through words, like in photographs, in paintings. Everything that has been forgotten. I am trying to write myself free, from darkness to clarity, to understanding.'

Photo: Raija Luukkonen

Anne Hänninen

A flame of a maiden

A flame of a maiden sat on a mossy stone.
Against the stone, cartwheels were leaning:
like mild cows, with hearts of dandelion green.

All of a sudden, cartwheels became years of tomorrow,
they tumbled to slush.

Of a sudden, wheels everywhere, weird wheels:
well rings of let-down endlessly
spiralling towards the bottom.

And nobody's daughter peeped in there,
a daughter, not-of-her-life, looked, saw the rings,
they brought dear memories.

And a daughter, not-of-herself, touched the wheels:
blood sprayed from the fingers!

The mossy stone slid away
the grass swayed.

Geometric figures filled all —
transfers, projections, scraps,
tricks, shadowgraphs, puns.

In my girlish summers

In my girlish summers there were bumblebees,
shrill crickets, sweet butterflies.

And wild strawberries, cornflowers,
the needless glow of colours.

Earth was always soft under a bare foot,
my mind, light cloudlets in the sky.

The summers were long, throbbing sun-bosoms.

The smell of silken meadows reached the bed at night.
My skin breathed like a rose.

I wonder if anyone saw that tree

I wonder if anyone saw that tree
in the same way as I,
uniquely.

We could meet in that tree
in the clarity of understanding?

Circus vans arrive

Circus vans arrive showering cat's gold, blinding.
The vans I'm waiting for will never arrive!
I'm alone in the forest of clouds, of ambushers.
I cannot play with hearts! Not today, nor tomorrow!
I need immaterial light to blow me into dance,
I need it, I'm thirsting!
What am I doing in moribund brown!
I don't want to eat the fruit of evil from these trees!
Unselfish storm, fell the trees if, in the land of chameleons,
even one of them won't change its colour, into a lasting
serenity of wisdom, if the shadows of suffering cast
    by the knives of wrath
won't run away, won't run away by now! If nights won't fall!
If the heart-crushing circus won't end!

Do I have to eat the fruit of evil in order to live?
Isn't there anything else, won't there ever be anything else?

No, I have to eat it
in order to die.

The hand of the clock

The hand of the clock pounds, leaps into emptiness.
Timelessness ticks.

There's a grease spot in the cousin's graduation photo,
on the walls, works by the artist who died in the dump.

Death ticks more loudly than a clock or a heart.

Death will always reach its goal.

The wind will sweep away consoling flowers from the graves,
in faceless moonlights, anonymity will wail.

The clock undresses me, ticking, my chameleon layers fall,
clear colours mix as if I were
an aquarelle having drowned, among aquarelles and
when it pours with rain.

Marshlands of mist, inexplicable forms,
a strange mute wind goes through the clock, pictures, and me.

There's nothing to say.
A cool waste land, nudeness.

Where are you man

Where are you man, paramount to your original?

I'm looking for you, endlessly.

You're not borne by the earth sunken in sickness,
    nor by the mother in chains.
Nor can black waves form your figure from the foam.

You are not brought to mountains, valleys, by rusty grey
                                                    clouds.
Nor are you borne by the fire of war, no!

In vain I cry for you, new man, like the dawn,
as the morning awakening on the lap of roses, without
                                                    danger.

Only an image you are, new man, in dreams, at times,
and while awake, such a stranger.

Many a man, cool and empty

Many a man, cool and empty, fears to bathe himself
in the foam of feeling, in the shower of thought.

He's afraid of the light piercing through,
of dancing among mulleins, like bees madly swooning.

He doesn't want to grow into a bird of light, into a velvet rose,
blooming boldly, humbly, rising for ever
towards the more beautiful . . .

He doesn't want to step on sunbeams: only then
could he embrace everything.
And he doesn't feel a great love
that could extinguish all lustre.

This is enough for him, cool and empty:
his coolness, emptiness.

Annukka

Peura

Born 1st March, 1968, in Turku. Was
awarded the J.H. Erkko Prize for the
best poetry début in 1989. Studies
literature, philosophy and Japanese at
the University of Helsinki.

*'My first book, 'The Passenger of Chaos', was published in 1989.
I was then 21. The book was a result of a gruelling, fast-lane life,
although at bottom – as one of my friends described it – my life
seems to be permeated by happiness. I chose poetry as my
medium of expression, because it fitted best with what a book
claims to be. My literary forefathers and mothers have been
Sylvia Plath, Sappho, Marcel Proust and some wonderful
chosen Finnish poets.*

*As a writer and as a person I am moving to new regions of
experience, while saying good-bye to old ones. My former
interest in Asian, particularly Japanese literature, is now giving
way to an interest in Europe: modern French thought and
literature, ancient Greek poetry, feminist criticism, mythology
. . . I have faith in European ways of thought; as a European I
want to know my background, its movements and dimensions.
Asia is another dimension, not buried or forgotten, but at the
moment latent, for me. A writer is a citizen of the mind, who has
the chance of freedom – mentally, if not always physically.
Intellectual passion makes this chance real. I imagine that in the
realm of the word, a writer is given, not a passport, but a* passe-
partout*: a universal key, a folding cardboard frame for defining
things, and a pass that is valid everywhere!'*

Annukka Peura

When the man is fata morgana

When the man is fata morgana
and I, a fatalist
What could a poor sailor
name a ship:
'Reality that won't happen'?!

I didn't think of death

I didn't think of death when I bought my death's head ring
— just the smuggler's secret grave and tombstone came to
mind,

Skull & Crossbones, in the South of England

and the smiling salesgirl,
with high cheekbones
and trumpets of inflorescence in her lap.
Her name was
                    Bindweed

I'll bury the bones

I'll bury the bones of your face.
What I have seen,
    and the hare's shriek against the distancing sky,
    how suddenly the animal shook off from it.

SO SO

Finally I could roll
a bird into my lap, a diminishing bird perspective.

But what trembled on my knee,
was a bird-shaped thread.

You didn't take the challenge,
you wanted this, you wanted that,
so so

    even your shirt was lost in the grass

Now you can speak!
    start, let's say, with my eyes
        they're green, too
        and here's your shirt

        peterpan

I was looking for the company of roses

I was looking for the company of roses
when I noticed: the centre of the rose
is a labyrinth.
I walked out of my house.
On the threshold I met you.

The passenger of Chaos

The passenger of Chaos could choose an instrument:
he chose a tin flute.
He would have liked to choose the guitar,
but the instrument had been taken already, of course.
He doesn't know how to play, he doesn't even know how to
read the score!
But again and again he succeeds in being caught by the
dream hold.

— The man told his story which had no place for Chance.
He spoke fast, but the passenger of Chaos captured him
and stood there waiting at the story's end.
The man never got there.
He carried the words from his mouth to another town
and the other guitar, his own,
the one that held its string out in the wind
the one that spoke darkly, he left under the bridge of
sighs

I've seen the world's most beautiful violin case

I've seen the world's most beautiful violin case.
It's made of the tree of the wooden clogs,
                its hinges of lace-metal.
The man laid down the case
and thought he would free his hands.
He carved his initials on the top and came to tell
me: This is a ship.
This is Mine he said.
Then the wind grabbed his hair and sped him away.

I didn't lean on any one
when I looked, look:
a guitar lies inside the violin case. A red
guitar, not meant to be played.
I knew it from the start.

Lo bueno y lo malo

You're the Holy Blood
in me, Baby
It's true, you're my blood and my wine,
    good blood
    and Big Bad Blood! I'm not afraid

Even when very young   I was passed the essence
       of the Holy Grail,
   far-sighted, not forgotten
   and on the Grail a patchwork of questions
                        (a wedding cloth,
                        a bread cloth)::
   Where did it come from
   and what did it contain,
   whose hands offered it to drink?
                  (Who dunnit, Who?)

Other Scandinavian Titles Published by Forest Books

PREPARATIONS FOR FLIGHT & OTHER SWEDISH STORIES

Translated by Robin Fulton

Robin Fulton, one of the best-known translators of contemporary Swedish literature, has gathered a collection of stories which, as he says in his preface, remained in his mind long after a first reading. In all of them, concrete reality evokes mystery, and in many of them, childhood reflections affect and are affected by everyday adult experience.

ISBN 0 948259 66 3   paper £8.95   176pp

SPRING TIDE

by Pia Tafdrup

Translated from the Danish by Anne Born

Spring Tide is a book about desire, about woman's passion. From inception through total immersion in sensual emotion towards an apprehension of winter's cold, Pia Tafdrup links personal ecstasy with the cyclic rhythm of life. Hailed by Scandinavian critics as a young Danish poet of exceptional talent, Pia Tafdrup, in this sustained sequence of thought-provoking poems, turns language into experience.

ISBN 0 948259 55 8   paper £6.95   96pp

Hour of the Lynx

A play by Per Olov Enquist

Translated by Ross Shideler

A young boy is committed to a psychiatric institution for a motiveless murder. A sensitive and challenging play, *The Hour of the Lynx* focuses on the boy's role in a controlled experiment in which the researcher gives him a cat to care for. The pastor and the researcher struggle to understand the boy's complex emotional riddles which ultimately reveal profound insights into the mystery and miracle of love and salvation. Enquist is one of Scandinavia's foremost dramatists; productions of his work in Scandinavian and European theatres have established him as a leading European writer.

ISBN 0 948259 85 X   paper £6.95   64pp

The Seer
and Other Norwegian Stories

by Jonas Lie

Translated by Brian Morton
& Richard Trevor

Trolls or unconscious impulses? Jonas Lie, Norway's great nineteenth century writer, had by his own admission, a twilight nature. Like the landscape, it shifted from light to dark in a fantastic world of superstition. *The Seer* and eight other shorter stories reveal the progress over a period of time towards that darkening vision – towards the belief that within each one of us there is a small, exciting and incalculable troll.

ISBN 0 948259 65 5   paper £8.95   160pp

SNOW AND SUMMERS

by Solveig von Schoultz

Translated from the Swedish by Anne Born

Snow and Summers presents the cream of von
Schoultz's poetry from almost fifty years for the first
time in English. 'For both poet and reader', writes Bo
Carpelan, 'von Schoultz's poetry is an exercise in the
sharpening of vision . . . sincerity and smiling wis-
dom engendered by a lifetime of experience.'

ISBN 0 948259 52 3   paper £7.95   128pp

HEARTWORK

by Solveig von Schoultz

Translated from the Swedish
by Marlaine Delargy & Joan Tate

Winner of numerous literary prizes, Solveig von
Schoultz is widely acknowledged as one of Finland's
leading poets and prose writers. 'Her short stories',
writes Bo Carpelan, present an acute and subtle
analysis of human relationships – between adults
and children, men and women, and between different
generations . . . She is not only a listener and an
observer: she is also passionately involved with these
dramas of everyday life which are all concerned with
the problems of human value and human growth.
These she portrays without sentimentality but with
the rich perception of experience.'

ISBN 0 948259 50 7   paper £7.95   144pp

ROOM WITHOUT WALLS

Selected poems of Bo Carpelan

Translated from the Swedish by Anne Born

Perhaps the greatest poet writing in Finland today, Bo Carpelan takes much of his inspiration from the landscape of Finland, its stern northern wintry presence and its delicate spring and summer. In style concise, pure and clear, in form economical, he writes with a delicate lyrical beauty of fundamental human experience. Beneath the spare, deceptively simple surface lie vast eternities, gentle echoes, mysteries, sorrows, signs and warnings.

ISBN 0 948259 08 6   paper £6.95   144pp illustrated

THE NAKED MACHINE

Poems by Matthías Johannessen

Translated by Marshall Brement

This is the first volume of a contemporary Icelandic poet to be published in English. Already translated into many languages, Matthías Johannessen is acknowledged as one of Iceland's greatest living poets. The translator, Marshall Brement, is also a poet and met Johannessen while American Ambassador to Iceland.

ISBN 0 948259 43 4   paper £5.95   96pp illustrated
ISBN 0 948259 44 2   cloth £7.95   96pp illustrated